Angels in the Kitchen

Angels in the Kitchen

ONE HUNDRED PIECES OF
CHILDHOOD WISDOM

Compiled by
JILL WORTH

Hodder & Stoughton
LONDON SYDNEY AUCKLAND

British Library Cataloguing in Publication Data
A record for this book is available from
the British Library

ISBN 0 340 75619 5

Printed and bound in Great Britain
by Clays Ltd, St Ives plc

Hodder and Stoughton Ltd
A division of Hodder Headline
338 Euston Road
London NW1 3BH

Contents

Foreword

Children are many things: enchanting, exasperating, funny and often wise far beyond their years. Free from the burdens of social conventions that so frequently prevent adults saying what they really mean, children speak with an honesty that can be breathtaking.

This book is about just such sayings – the remarks or observations that made someone laugh, someone else wonder and yet another person struggle to hold back a tear. For children so often 'hit the nail on the head' and we, caught in the complexities of adulthood, mourn our own loss of such perception.

I am sure you like me have often heard

something said by a child and hoped not to forget it. The members of the Mothers' Union who have remembered and shared these childhood sayings deserve our thanks, as does Jill Worth who has compiled and fashioned this rich resource.

I asked a friend from my own childhood what was the most memorable thing her child had said to her. She answered, 'I love you.' As we read this book may we re-dedicate ourselves to the loving nurture of the next generation with whom we have so much to share and from whom so much to learn.

Lady Eames
World Wide President
of the Mothers' Union

Communion

My husband, as rural dean, took us all with him when he visited a church in his deanery. When it came to communion, this church used wafers rather than bread, which we used at our own church. When the wafer was raised at the appropriate time and broken in half, my youngest son said in a stage whisper: 'Doesn't that bread sound stale!'

Robert, aged three, on the way home from communion: 'Mummy, that was a lovely party. but who does the washing up?'

My three-year-old grandson Neil was having a conversation with his father.

DAD: What would you like to be when you grow up?

NEIL: A vicar.

DAD: What do vicars do?

NEIL: They give you round white things and say 'Bless your heart'.

DAD : What are these white things?

NEIL: They are from God, so you don't die.

A Catholic wedding with nuptial
mass, a full church, quiet with a
respectful hush. The priest
blessed the sacraments, then
drank from the wine, taking a
while to lower the chalice. A little
voice sang out: 'All gone!'

Our five-year-old son, on seeing across the communion rail an elderly gentleman wearing an eye-patch, said in a rather too loud voice: 'Look, Daddy, a real pirate!'

The Sunday school children had been shown the various parts of the church and had been told the name of each. Some time later, in order to see how much they remembered, they were asked the names of the various parts.

When they came to the altar rail, where unconfirmed children come to receive a blessing during the communion, there was a blank silence as to its name. Eventually, one little boy suggested: 'Is it called the blessing bar?'

We took our five-year-old granddaughter to a communion service. Victoria kneeled obediently at the altar rail and the vicar, holding a piece of bread in his hand ready for the next communicant, put his hand on her head and blessed her. As we walked back down the aisle, Victoria turned to me and asked in a loud voice: 'Why did the vicar put a crumb on my head?'

When taking our four-year-old granddaughter Eleanor to a communion service for the first time, she became very worried and held on to my hand. Looking very upset, she said: 'Nan, I don't have to drink the blood, do I?'

All of the family gathered in church for my youngest granddaughter's christening. At communion, the children were invited to go to the altar rail with their parents. Jonathan, aged nine, went with his mother, and on return asked, 'Granny, why did that lady put her hand on my head?'

I replied, 'She was saying, "God bless you".'

A slight pause, then Jonathan said, 'But Granny, I didn't sneeze!'

During communion, my daughter took her two small girls to the altar rail for a blessing. My youngest granddaughter took her favourite toy with her, but returned to their pew in tears. 'Alex, he didn't do my dolly,' whispered the two-year-old. Her sister replied, 'Never mind, Joey. We'll do it ourselves when we get home.'

The Church Service

On our way to a church service, my granddaughter Ruby, aged three, took my hand and said, 'Grandma, when the vicar says our prayers we must all kneel down and say out loud, "Old Men".' When we arrived at church and looked round the assembled congregation, I couldn't help but think she had a good point.

When my grandson was about three and a half years old, he stopped overnight with me and I took him to church the next morning. I kept looking at him now and again, and could see he was sitting very quietly and seeming to take it all in. But as soon as our vicar had finished the sermon, he turned to me and exclaimed, 'That was *so* boring, Nanny!'

On being led out of church for Sunday school, our three-year-old daughter announced: 'I know why we have to be quiet as we go out.'

'Oh, why is that?' asked her mum.

'So we don't wake up the adults!' she replied.

During a service, I was surprised that my three-year-old daughter sat quite still and listened to all that was said. Then suddenly she boldly stood up and said, 'Thank you God, Amen. May I please leave the table?'

Mixed-up Words

The reader at the church service came to the end of the reading and said, 'For the Word of the Lord . . .' and the people responded, 'Thanks be to God.'

'Oh, so *that's* Peter God!' piped up my small granddaughter.

My four-year-old grandson came back into church for the weekly 'tell the congregation what you've done in junior church this morning'. They all lined up and our vicar asked what they'd been learning about this week. Silence and foot shuffling. Had it been about John the Baptist? More silence. Well, had he done something special to Jesus? More silence, then with great confidence and aplomb, my grandson beckoned the vicar to bring over the microphone. Loud and clear he announced: 'He hypnotised him!'

Some years ago in Easter week, many of our family were gathered for my parents' Golden Wedding. The children decided to act the Passion story. All went well until my seven-year-old niece came running in to greet the risen Lord. With a dazzling smile, she cried, 'Ribena!'

My mother's youngest sister, when she was seven years old, was asked by her mother to repeat the Bible verse she had learned at school that week. She replied: 'The birds of the air have their nests, but the Son of God has nowhere to lay his eggs.'

PRIEST: The Lord be with you.

MY VERY SMALL SON: And with high spirits.

Five-year-old Tom was saying prayers with his daddy. He asked to say 'the fellowship prayer', which was his name for 'the grace'. Daddy asked him if he knew what 'grace' was; he didn't, so his father tried to explain. Then Tom was asked if he knew what 'fellowship' meant. 'Oh, yes,' said Tom confidently. 'It's that fellow's ship who was eaten by a big fish and sicked up later.'

The Lord's Prayer

When my husband's work took him to Llandovery, he moved there ahead of me and the children. Temporarily homeless, I moved in with my parents in Cardiff. We all missed Daddy very much, especially my two-year-old. One evening, when we were saying bedtime prayers together, he clasped his hands together and said, 'Our Father, has gone to Llandovery.'

By the age of three, our daughter
Andrea could say most of the
Lord's Prayer. Sitting up in bed,
eyes closed and hands clasped,
she said: 'Our Father, in charge of
heaven . . . ' I found it difficult to
correct her, for after all, she had
got it right.

My young friend Richard was delighted to tell his mother how important his name was, as the Lord's Prayer began: 'Our Father Richard in heaven . . . '

The Lord's Prayer, by my four-year-old grandson: 'Our Father, I was in heaven, Harold is your name, Forgive us our trespasses as we forgive those who trip along.'

Hymns and Songs

Did you know that the Teletubbies had made it into the hymnbook? My five-year-old son came home from school singing, 'Go, Teletubby mountain'.

My four-year-old grandson was at church with his family when the hymn 'Let's celebrate' was announced. My son and daughter-in-law suddenly realised he was singing, 'Come on, let's Sellotape, Sellotape, Sellotape and string.'

'Jesus' blood was shed for me' sang the congregation. My four-year-old grandson asked in a quiet pause, 'Where did he have his shed?' To his father's 'I'll explain later' he insisted: 'What would he keep in a shed? Did he have a bicycle?' The congregation had to finish their laughter before the service could continue.

Many years ago our eight-year-old daughter Alison returned from Sunday school and announced they had been singing 'our' hymn. Her dad and I couldn't think who would have writen a hymn for us. Then she began to sing 'Jesus, good above all other . . . Give us grace to *persevere*.' Our names are Percy and Vera!

We were travelling in the car with my mother and our three children. Our eldest son, quite deaf at the time, was rendering the latest song he'd heard at Sunday school. My mother remarked on the painful sound he was making, only to be met with the reply: 'Well, *you* may not be enjoying it, Nanna, but *God* is!'

Prayer

When my son was five he jumped up and down with excitement when he woke up to find snow on the ground. 'I prayed for snow last night!' he announced. However, some hours later, our coal lorries, doing deliveries, became stuck in the snow, and his father had a job getting them on the road again. 'I didn't ask him to send *so* much,' said a sad little boy.

One Good Friday my husband took our five-year-old son Antony to bed and to hear his prayers. Antony began to pray, then stopped. My husband asked what was wrong. Antony replied: 'It's no good talking to Jesus today – he's dead and I can't talk to him again until Sunday.'

The Peace

At a family service, one little boy had a novel but very apt greeting during the Peace. While we were all shaking hands and saying, 'Peace be with you', he said, 'Pleased to be with you.'

One afternoon I was feeling unwell and went to sit on the sofa for a while. My three-year-old daughter Maria did not play with anything for more than a few moments, and I seemed to be constantly getting up to give her attention. After a while, in frustration, I said, 'You haven't given me any peace all afternoon.' Immediately she ran across the room, put her hands into mine and looking up at me said, 'Peace be with you, Mummy.' What else could I reply but, 'Peace be with you, Maria.'

The Vicar as God

My husband John, a retired Anglican priest, was acting as a locum for a colleague. One morning, when John was in the vestry, the door banged behind him and he found himself locked in the church. There he stayed for three hours before he was rescued by Anthony and his granny. Anthony's granny had explained to him that they were going to freshen the flowers in God's house. After John had thanked them and turned to go, he heard Anthony's high-pitched voice: 'Why was God locked in his house, Granny? Hasn't he got another key?'

As I left church with my four-year-old granddaughter, who was staying with me, I explained to the vicar that Chanel was visiting, but actually lived in Blackburn. The vicar said he used to live in Blackburn, but now lives in Freckleton. When we arrived home, Chanel told her daddy, 'Do you know that God used to live in Blackburn, but now he lives here with Grandma?'

One Sunday, when the vicar of a nearby church was ill, the assistant priest from our own church deputised for him. Later that day, the four-year-old boy from next door who attends that church came to our house to play. He told me he liked going to church 'because God is there'. He continued: 'But he was sick today so we had to get a new one!'

When we left church my four-year-old granddaughter said sadly, 'God didn't say good morning to me, did he?'

'I'm sure he did,' I replied, 'because he's everywhere. Maybe he said it quietly and you didn't hear.'

'No, he didn't,' she persisted. 'But he said good morning to you and you shook his hand!'

I explained to our new little foster child that we were going to church on Sunday. She had obviously never been to church before and asked why we were going. I told her we were going to learn all about God.

'Oh!' she said excitedly, 'I know him!'

Intrigued, I asked her how she knew God.

She replied: 'He came to my old school once – I think it was for harvest!'

The Trinity . . .

Travelling on top of a London bus with my son, then aged six, we stopped outside a pawnbroker's shop. Simon noticed the three gold balls hanging there. 'What's that, Mum?' he asked. As I began to answer him, he announced, 'I know, it's Father, Son and Holy Spirit.'

. . . Father . . .

After searching for my four-year-old daughter for some time, I suddenly spotted her far in the distance, full of the joys of spring, across our field containing cattle. I shouted to her to return quickly.

'You must never go across the field on your own,' I told her when she returned. 'Always get Daddy or me to come with you.'

She answered with sincerity: 'But I wasn't on my own. God is in my heart!'

We were dairy farmers and when my son was four he won as a prize a book called *How God Made the World.* The centre-page spread was a farm scene with chickens, ducks, pigs and sheep running round the farmyard and cows looking over the fence. My son asked. 'Mummy, who milked the cows before God made the man?'

My friend Margaret was cleaning the church with help from her son Tom. After they had been busy for some time, Margaret noticed that Tom had disappeared. Telling herself not to panic – there are many hiding places in our church – she searched and called for him but the three-year-old was nowhere to be found. Then she noticed the altar cloth was moving, and lifted it to find Tom under the table

'What are you doing under there?' she cried.

An indignant voice replied, 'I'm playing hide and seek, and it's God's turn to find me.'

My six-year-old daughter and her friend were watching athletics, when the starter pistol was fired up into the air.

FRIEND: What would happen if it shot God?

MY DAUGHTER: I expect he'd rise again.

My three-and-a-half-year-old grandson and I were in church midweek, when no one else was there. While I was busy at the back of the church, Henry purposefully walked towards the altar, then looked in the chapel, then went up and down the aisles. He came back to me and said: 'God isn't at home. Perhaps he's gone shopping. Shall we wait for him, Grandma?'

Our grandson Robert, aged four, asked his mother: 'Who borned God?'

On hearing his daddy telling him that 'God is great', my three-year-old son Richard said, 'No, he isn't.'

But his six-year-old brother Martin responded, 'Of course he is – he must be, because Jesus sat on his right hand.'

I bought a new tennis ball for my grandson, Lee. As he tossed it from hand to hand, he said thoughtfully, 'I can't give *this* back to God.' Then, looking up at the sky, 'I couldn't throw it that far.'

. . . Son . . .

I was walking home from church with my seven-year-old daughter. 'I didn't know they had aeroplanes when Jesus lived here,' she said.

'They didn't,' I replied.

'Well then,' she retorted, 'why did the vicar say he was a lover of concord?'

When my grandson Ben was three years old, I took him to morning worship. Thoughtfully he looked up at the high vaulted roof and asked in a loud voice, 'Granny, is that Jesus's bedroom?'

'Grandma, I've got a surprise for you, and you're going to be very excited,' announced my four-year-old grandson Stephen. 'All those bad men who killed Jesus, who made him die on the cross – well, that happened a long, long time ago, so they're all dead now. They aren't here any more!'

As I faced my new class of six-year-olds, I smiled encouragingly and said, 'You are going to have a great treat now as I am going to tell you a story. And the story is about Jesus.'

A hand shot up at the back of the class. On enquiry, I received the very polite statement: 'Mrs White, we *did* Jesus with Mrs Andrews last year!'

When my nephew was two, we were looking through a catalogue, discussing what he would like for Christmas. As I turned to a page of musical equipment, he pointed to a guitar and told me he wanted an 'electric Jesus'. I discovered later from his father that he thought a guitar was called a 'Jesus' because every time he went to a Pram Service and people stood up to talk about Jesus, they always sang songs to the accompaniment of electric guitars.

Walking to church one morning, we explained to our three-year-old that we were going to God's house. He obviously thought about this during the service. When we came to the end of a hymn, his voice was heard: 'Is that Jesus up there playing the piano?' He knew Jesus was God's son, so it was reasonable he might be playing the piano in God's house.

When our granddaughter was nearly five, she told us: 'Today we learned about Jesus turning water into wine, but I've forgotten how you do it.'

. . . and Holy Spirit . . .

Oliver, aged three, asked, 'Mummy, you know when a lady is pregnant? Has she got two Holy Spirits inside her?'

Bedtime prayers

During bedtime prayers, my four-year-old son Joshua came out with this profound and challenging prayer: 'Lord Jesus, please help those people with rusty hearts.'

Our four-year-old daughter was saying her bedtime prayers: 'Dear God, I hope you are all right up there with all those dead people.'

After our youngest son was diagnosed profoundly deaf after meningitis at five months, I was determined that we would continue to communicate. Thanks to a peripatetic teacher, we learned to sign together. On the first hot night of summer, when he was looking forward to wearing a pair of new shorts the next morning, four-year-old Thomas signed his usual 'God bless Mummy and Daddy, Matthew and Daniel' then lay back with a happy sigh and added 'and God bless little trousers.'

We were spending a few days with my parents, but my husband was unable to be with us. At bedtime I suggested to my daughter Sheila, then aged two, that we said a special prayer for Daddy at home. Eyes closed, hands together, she commenced: 'Please God, look after . . .' Then in an aside whisper to me, she asked, 'Does God call him Daddy or John?'

Libby, my five-year-old granddaughter, was saying her bedtime prayers. 'Dear God, will you please look after all the people in Kosovo and keep them safe? Dear God, in my class there are thirteen girls and only five boys. Could you please send some more boys so that we all have a boy each? Dear God, will you please look after Auntie Mary and make her better, so that when I meet her in town she will give me £1? Amen.'

Death and Heaven

My young son had a great interest in miniature steam models operated by methylated spirit. One day a funeral cortege passed us, the first my son had seen. He wanted to know what it was, and I tried to explain that someone had died and was to be buried. He seemed quite bothered about that, so I added that their spirit had gone to heaven. 'Mum,' he asked after a few moments of reflection, 'do you mean methylated spirit?'

My daughter and I were discussing the death of two friends. Miriam, my three-year-old granddaughter, who had obviously been listening to the conversation, came over to me and sat on my knee. 'Grandmas don't die, do they?' she asked.

'When you go to heaven,' announced my five-year-old daughter Jessie, 'you can take your shoes and socks off and run through the big fluffy clouds without falling through!'

An archaeological dig was taking place near our home, and I took my five-year-old grandson Ben to a museum where the findings – including some skeletons – were being displayed. As we left and were crossing the churchyard, he turned to me and said, 'Grandma, you know when you die and go to Jesus – well, you only take your skin!'

Tom, my grandson, was exceptionally short-sighted. When he was four, he said: 'When I die, I hope I am wearing my glasses, because I don't want to miss seeing Jesus.'

My granddaughter Emma, aged four, enjoys looking at a photo of my husband. She accepts that Grandpa has gone to live with Jesus, and won't come back. One day, while her mother was cooking the lunch, Emma was talking into her pretend mobile phone. Her mother asked who was phoning, and she said: 'It's Grandpa. He's quite all right.' Then she went on: 'Do you know, Mummy, Jesus has cooked his lunch already!'

When my granddaughter was two and a half, her pet guinea pig gave birth to stillborn babies. Laura was very distressed by this, and suggested phoning Monica, her Sunday school teacher. Her mum explained that Monica was not at home. 'Let's ring God then,' Laura pleaded.

I heard two children in my infant class talking.

'My granddad's gone to heaven.'

'Is he really dead?'

'No, he isn't dead, he's living there – my mother said.'

My grandson Ben, aged four, asked: 'Do they have toys in heaven or do you have to take your own?'

FOUR-YEAR-OLD TOM: Jonathan, do you think there will be Lego in heaven?

SIX-YEAR-OLD JONATHAN: I don't know, but keep a few pieces in your pocket just in case.

Angels

My daughter said to her son Ben, 'Talk to Neil (then three months old) in the kitchen while I hang out the washing.' A few minutes later Ben followed his mummy into the garden, saying, 'The angels are in the kitchen – they will talk to Neil.'

Our headmaster frequently used a prayer that sounded like, 'Therefore with angels and half angels'. I pictured an angel with only half a body under the white gown, who had been punished for not being as good as the other angels. Perhaps not-so-good people were cut in half when they went to heaven? I was very relieved when I discovered the correct word was 'archangel'.

Christmas

My elder son, aged five, when asked why we should go to church on Christmas Day, replied: 'I expect people to come to my house on my birthday, so we ought to go to Jesus' house on his.'

As head of an infant department I ensured that all two hundred children had an active part in our Nativity performance. Each child had been told which part they were to play, and at the first practice, I was positioning them in the hall.

'Angels over there . . . Shepherds . . . Wise Men . . . Mary and Joseph . . .'

One five-year-old was totally lost. 'Billy, who are you?' I asked.

'I don't know. I think I'm a book.'

A book? Looking quickly down the list of characters, I discovered he was playing the part of a page!

It was the Carol Service and the church was packed. There had just been a reading in which the angel told Mary she was to have a child, and this was followed by a time of silent prayer. Sarah, aged two and a half, in a very loud stage whisper, broke the silence: 'Mummy, how *did* Jesus get into his mummy's tummy?'

When my three-year-old grand-daughter Miriam was talking about baby Jesus, shortly after Christmas, she said: 'His mother was Mary, his father was Joseph. That's Mr and Mrs Christ and their baby Jesus.'

When I provided the doll for our crib in the church, one young member of the congregation was not impressed. During the Christmas morning service young Emma announced: 'Huh! That's not baby Jesus, it's got two teeth!'

A child in my infant class was unimpressed by Mary and Joseph having nowhere to stay. It was their own fault, he decided, because '*my* dad would have booked'.

Our rector is often invited to the local nursery school plays at Christmas time. He has come to realise that not all the words of the teacher's script, so faithfully learnt, have meaning to young children. In particular, he remembers one small Joseph knocking on the innkeeper's door and enquiring loudly: 'Have you any room in your bin?'

My twin godchildren were ecstatic when they were given important parts in the infants' Nativity play. Charlie was the innkeeper and Ellie was chosen to be Mary. All went well until Joseph knocked on the door of the inn and requested a room for the night

'Of course,' said Charlie, 'please come in.'

Afterwards we asked Charlie why he'd deviated from the script.

'Well,' he said, 'my sister didn't have her sleep this afternoon, and she's very tired.'

On the Christmas Eve before her third birthday, after I had put our daughter Penny to bed, I could still hear her voice. I looked in to see if anything was wrong. 'I'm all right, Mummy, I'm just having a chat with God,' she said. I said goodnight again, then paused on the landing to hear, 'So please God, give us a good day tomorrow. What would Jesus think if it rained on his birthday?'

Easter

During Holy Week, my nephew was taking his four-year-old daughter through all the events of Easter. When it came to Good Friday, he did his best to explain about the death of Jesus. His daughter looked puzzled and was obviously turning things over in her mind. Then she said, 'He didn't live long, did he? He was only born at Christmas!'

At Easter, seven-year-old Alexander announced: 'All is well in heaven now. Joseph was a good stepfather, but now Jesus is in heaven with God his father and his mother Mary.'

My four-year-old granddaughter, Rebecca, had been learning about Easter gardens at play school. Obviously this included a *Blue Peter*-type demonstration using a yoghurt container with two divisions. When her mother met her at the end of the morning and they were discussing the day's activities, Rebecca said seriously: 'Did you know that Jesus was buried in a yoghurt pot?'

The Old Testament

Our five-year-old was reading the creation story in a children's Bible. 'And God saw what he had made, and it was . . .' Michael looked up at the page-turn and said, 'such fun!'

OLIVER (AGED FIVE): It's not fair on the people born after Moses.

MUM: Why not?

OLIVER: Well, we all have to obey the Ten Commandments, but all those people born before Moses didn't have to bother.

When my grandson was a toddler, he was happily crayoning in his book during the sermon, when he suddenly tried to take his sandals off.

'What are you doing?' my daughter whispered.

'The man told us to take our sandals off,' he replied.

Sure enough, the rector was quoting from Exodus 3, the story of Moses and the burning bush, and my grandson had acted quite literally on hearing, 'Take off your sandals because you are standing on holy ground.'

And Finally . . .

In the 1960s, our vicar wisely decided to involve our very active son David in some activity rather than asking him to sit quietly through the service. First it was the choir, then one day he ran into the house and breathlessly announced that the vicar had asked him to be a server. I said I didn't think he could do that until he was confirmed.

'Oh, but it's all right,' said David. 'The vicar says he will bless me for a week or two.'

We all thought that he well might!

Some thirty-odd years ago, when my husband was churchwarden and I was leader of the Ladies' Fellowship, we had an interregnum and were both very busy at the church. The area where we were living was in uproar – there were blue vans and gas pipes everywhere. One day the doorbell rang and our daughter answered.

'Good morning,' said the man at the door. 'I called about converting you to natural gas.'

'No, thank you,' said Sue. 'We have enough trouble in this house with the Church of England!' and closed the door.

Our grandson Matthew, aged six, who worships in one of the parish churches of which my husband is the rector and I am the curate, told our Sunday club leader, 'I think you ought to know that Mr Luff is my grandfather in real life.'

My nephew announced that he would like to be a writer when he left school. His parents told him that many people write books, but few can make a living from it. His six-year-old brother declared: 'When I leave school I'm going to write Bibles, because they always sell.'

In 1790, Peter Taylor bought a family Bible which was to be handed down to the descendants of the same name. Eventually my husband inherited it, and when our son was born, he was given the family name.

When my son was seven years old, granddad came to visit, which meant there were three Peters in the house. Someone shouted 'Peter!'

My son answered crossly, saying: 'From now on I want to be called Simon.'

'Why Simon?' we said.

Surprised, he said, 'Simon called Peter of course!'

After attending Sunday school on the first Sunday in Lent, five-year-old Fiona went to play with her friend Vanessa. Fiona was explaining to her friend that the class had been encouraged to give up something they really enjoy, such as chocolate, in the weeks leading up to Easter.

VANESSA: What will you give up?

FIONA: I don't know.

VANESSA: You could give up drawing and colouring.

FIONA: I know – I'll give up Sunday school!

My eight-year-old friend Andre, chatting in my kitchen, suddenly said: 'You go to church, don't you? I want to be Christianed.' Knowing he was not christened, I said, 'That's good, Andre,' and began to explain that he would need to attend classes from the vicar

'I don't want to go to lessons – it's bad enough going to school,' he replied. So I asked him why he wanted to be christened. He said: 'Because I don't want to be married in a registry office.'

My godson was very interested in the Sunday school lesson which taught the importance of sharing. One day, on returning from work, his father was dismayed to find his son on the floor of the study, surrounded by the contents of one of his desk drawers – calculator, pens, accounts, papers . . .

'What do you think you're doing? Leave those things alone at once,' cried Dad.

My godson very calmly regarded his father and sighed, 'You know your trouble, Dad? You've got to learn to share.'

For my sister's sixtieth birthday, the whole family went out for a bar lunch. Elizabeth, her youngest granddaughter, was six years old and had never been out for a celebration like this, only having had parties at home. The following day at Sunday school, she heard the story of Lazarus being raised from the dead. Coming home, she told her grandma all about it, and finished the story by saying: 'Lazarus was so pleased he wasn't dead that he said, "Shall we celebrate and have a bar lunch?"'

My young daughter, when a new family moved into our village, said: 'Do they go to church or do they go to car boot sales?'

As a supervisor of school lunches in the reception class, it was my custom to say grace before the children opened their lunchboxes. On the first day of a new intake, I explained to the children what we were going to do. I then prayed: 'Thank you God for our food, for our families and for our friendships. Amen.'

The children began to tuck into their lunch, all except for Andrew, whose lunchbox remained unopened. When I asked him why he wasn't eating his lunch, he replied: 'You said, "Thank you God for the chips," so I'm waiting for the chips to come.'

When I worked in a children's home, I borrowed a van and took some of the smaller children for a day by the sea. Returning home, the sky became as black as ink, and the children thought we would not be able to find our way home. Suddenly an orange glow appeared in the sky straight ahead, and one of the five-year-olds said: 'Look! God has drawn his curtains to show us the way home!'

One Sunday my five-year-old daughter returned home from Sunday school very impressed with that morning's story of the Good Samaritan. A few weeks later, our vicar was telling the same story as part of his sermon. The congregation was quiet and receptive as he told of the man lying by the side of the road, passed by once, passed by twice . . .

Suddenly my daughter leapt up and cried out: 'Don't worry, don't worry. The ambulance comes along in a minute!'